A Critical Analysis of Vijay Tendulkar's

Sakharam Binder

Dr. Beena A. Mahida

CANADIAN

Academic Publishing

2014

Price : $27.86

First Edition : December, 2014

ISBN :   978-1-926488-16-5

ISBN Allotment Agency : Library and Archives Canada (Govt. of Canada)

Published & Printed by
Canadian Academic Publishing
81, Woodlot Crescent,
Etobicoke,
Toronto, Ontario, Canada.
Postal Code- M9W 6T3
Phone- +1 (647) 633 9712
http://www.canadapublish.com

PREFACE

The tradition of Indian Drama is very old. It goes back to the Sanskrit Drama of ancient India. India being a large country with diverse cultures and regional languages has various traditions of form and matter, distinct and yet having many common factors of dramaturgy.

Drama in India has a long history and in regional languages it is as popular as other literary genres – fiction and poetry. In Indian Literature, drama in English has not attained much popularity because plays in regional languages dominate the theatre. In recent times, Plays in the regional languages are translated in to English and such translations have established link between East and West, and North and South as well as harmony and unity in modern India.

In this context Vijay Tendulkar's Marathi Plays occupy a unique place. When I read the English translation of Tendulkar's plays I decided to pursue my research on plays of Tendulkar and in this decision Dr.R.K.Madalia of the Department of English provided much needed help by accepting to become my Supervisor for the research. He suggested to carry out my research on Tendulkar's major 6 (six) plays and to analyse them from the point of view of characterization, themes and dramatic techniques. Each of the plays of Tendulkar presented new perspective which made stimulating reading.

Tendulkar has not contributed to the modern Marathi theatre but has given it a new dimension. His plays disturb the audience by raising complex issues that remain unsettled even today in modern India. Tendulkar is not feminist but women are at the center in his plays. He treats his women characters with understanding and compassion against men who are selfish and hypocritical.

I have tried my level best in analyzing the different aspects of Tendulkar's Plays yet I believe that literature offers vast spectrum and if something is left out in my research, I leave it to future scholars to pursue studies that are more elaborate. This book is slight modification of the thesis. I have separated each play for a separate book to get wider information regarding the play and the details within and tried to focus in details the themes, characters, and important aspects.

Sakharam Binder is probably Tendulkar's most intensely naturalistic play. Sakharam Binder was staged first on 10th March 1972. Following "The Vultures" (1970) which had ruffled middle-class sensibilities a bit, the play confirmed Tendulkar's image as a radical and iconoclastic dramatist. There was quite a storm with regard to the raciness of dialogue, the 'bold' portrayals of characters like Sakharam and Champa, and especially Sakharam's lashing out against the hypocrisy of people. Almost thirty five years later, what strikes one about the play is not so much the boldness of theme and character as the inner contradictions of the central character and the thematic confusion

The success or failure of any work of art depends upon its appeal – whether that appeal proves to be transitory or everlasting. A work of art with an everlasting appeal always remains eternal. It will not be out of the way or excessive exaggeration if the same thing is said about Tendulkar's plays.

Dr. Beena A. Mahida

CONTENTS

Preface

1.	Introduction	1 – 30
2.	Sakharam Binder : An Overview	31 – 33
3.	Manifestation of Violence in Human Being	34 – 38
4.	Manifestation of Physical Lust in Human Being	39 – 44
5.	Complexity of Human Mind	45 – 56
6.	Exploration of Marriage Institution Versus The Concept of Live-In-Relationship	57 – 65
7.	Dramatic Techniques in Sakharam Binder	66 – 69
8.	Conclusion	70 – 76
	Bibliography	

1. INTRODUCTION

Drama has always remained a unique means to spread morality and to entertain. Long before movies came into being Indian theatre had been a major source of spreading moral value and entertainment. The remarkable feature is that- in spite of the emergence of the Indian cinema, the Indian theatre has not lost significance.

The Indian cinema with all its advanced techniques, sophisticated cameras and freedom of variety has remained unsuccessful in surpassing the Indian Theatre. No doubt – an actor who works in a cinema gets more money than a player of the stage but- the player of the stage gets more appreciation than the actor on the screen. The camera of a movie allows the compensation of a re-take to the actor whereas for the artist of a theatre no re-take is possible. His work demands more sincerity and higher efficiency which finally bring greater appreciation to him.

The tradition of Indian Drama is very old. It goes back to the Sanskrit Drama of ancient India. India being a large country with diverse cultures and regional languages has various traditions of form and matter, distinct and yet having many common factors of dramaturgy. Modern Indian drama is influenced not only by classical Sanskrit drama or local folk forms but also by western theatre following the establishment of British rule in India.

N. S. Dharan, an eminent writer of Indian writing in English writes "Drama in India has a long history". Girish Karnad says that the earliest extant play in India was written as early as A.D. 200. Dating to the days of Bhasa, Bhavabuti and Kalidasa, drama can boast of a rich and chequered history. The early plays were written in Sanskrit, based on the Vedas and the Upanishads. In fact, the Vedas and the Upanishads have never ceased to be sources of inspiration to man of letters both in India and abroad. Down the centuries, Indian drama has undergone various metamorphoses and it still continues to flourish in all regional languages. In regional languages it enjoys almost an equal status along with two other major literary genres, namely fiction and poetry. In Indian literature drama in English is yet to register an appreciable growth. By and large, plays written in regional languages dominate the Indian theatre. These plays are easily intelligible to the audiences. Actors too can easily improvise in them.

Several regional amateur theatres have also flourished from time to time. In the post-Independence period, performing arts were employed as an effective means of public enlightenment during the First-Five year plan (1951-54). As a result the National school of Drama was established under the directorship Alkhazi. Institutions for training in dramatics were founded in big cities. Drama departments started functioning in several universities. The annual Drama Festival was started in New Delhi by the Sangit Natak Akademi in 1954. With so much encouragement coming from so many quarters, drama began to flourish in the regional languages.

During the last few years, several plays, originally written in the regional languages, have been translated into English. Today, a sizeable number of such plays do exist. According to many academicians, it is necessary to incorporate these translations into the corpus of Indian English Literature as they also contribute an important component to it. Such translations of plays have forged an effective link between the East and the West the North and the South of India and contributed, in no small measure, to the growing harmony and richness of contemporary creative consciousness.

According to **Indranath Chaudhary**, when the sahitya Akademi was set up in 1954, Dr. S. Radhakrishnan spelt out its objective as the promotion of the unity of Indian literature, despite India's geographical, political, Social, and Linguistic diversities. Dr. Radhakrishnan gave a slogan to the Akademi that Indian literature is one, though written in many languages. It is in this context that the plays of Girish Karnad in Kannada, Mohan Rakesh in Hindi, Badal Sircar in Bengali and Vijay Tendulkar in Marathi occupy a unique place as pointed out by **Arundhati Banerjee** :

"In the 1960s four dramatisls from different regions of India writing in their own regional languages were said to have ushered modernity in to the sphere of Indian drama and theatre. They were Mohan Rakesh in Hindi, Badal Sircar in Bengali and Vijay Tendulkar in Marathi and Girish Karnad in Kannada. Rakesh's untimely death left his life's work incomplete, and Karnad has written only intermittently. Sircar, of course, has been almost as active as Tendulkar though his plays can be divided in to three distinct periods. Tendulkar, however, has not only been the most productive but has also introduced the greatest variations in his dramatic creations."

V. B. Deshpande rightly states, "Since the Independence – since 1950, to be precise – the name of Vijay Tendulkar has been in the forefront of the Marathi drama and stage. His personality both as man and writer is multifaceted. It has often been puzzling and curious with a big question mark on it. In the last 55 years he has written stories, novels, one – act plays, plays for children as well adults. Similarly he has done script6 writing and news paper columns as well. And in all these fields he has created an image of his own. Thus he is a creative writer with a fine sensibility and at the same time a contemplative and controversial dramatist. He has made a mark in the field of journalism also. Because of his highly individual viewpoint and vision of life and because of his personal style of writing he has made a powerful impression in the field of literature and drama, and has given the post-independence, Marathi drama a new idiom. By doing this he has put Marathi drama on the national and international Map."

The same indebtedness is expressed by **Arundhati Banerjee** "Vijay Tendulkar has been in the vanguard of not just Marathi but Indian theatre for almost forty years".He not only pioneered the experimental theatre movement in Marathi but also guided it."

While talking about contemporary Marathi Theatre **Dhyaneshwar Nadkarni** points out,

"Vijay Tendulkar leads the vanguard of the avant garde theatre that developed as a movement separate from the mainstream. Tendulkar and his colleagues were dissatisfied with the decadent professional theatre that characterized the Thirties and Forties. They wanted to give theatre a new form and therefore experimented with all aspects of it including content, acting décor and audience communication."

Chandrasekhar Barve expresses a similar opinion about Tendulkar's contribution to Marathi theatre,

"We can say with certainty that Tendulkar has guided Marathi drama that seemed to have lost its proper track, and has kept leading it for over two decades. His place and importance in this respect shall remain unique in the history of Marathi drama.

There may be controversies regarding his greatness but his achievements are beyond question.

He has written 28 full length plays, 24 one-act plays, several middles, articles, editorials and 11 plays for children. In spite of his success in every genre, his versatility as a writer has been overshadowed by his fame as a dramatist since drama has been his forte.

Mr. Barve observes,

"His extra-dramatic writing also reveals his pure taste for drama which tries to capture the different tensions and through them, finds "dramatics" accurately".His one-act plays are more experimental than his full-length plays. Most of them have been translated and produced in major Indian languages and some of them into English.

Vijay Tendulkar was born in **1928** at **Bombay** in **Maharastra**. He was born and brought up in Kandevali, a small lane in Girgaon. A lower middle class community dwelt. There and the males were mostly the shopkeepers and clerks. He was living in a typical chawl, in apartments of one room, kitchen, balcony and common toilets, so Tendulkar's upbringing in a lower middle class community provided him chance to perceive middle class minutely which helped him to portray its different shades on the stage.

His **father Mr. Dhondopant Tendulkar** was a head clerk at a British publishing firm called Longmans Green and company (Now Orient Longman). His **mother Mrs. Susheela Tendulkar** was a housewife. His father was a writer, director and actor of amateur Marathi plays. He didnot join the commercial drama company as formerly a career in the theatre was not honoured. Four years old Tendulkar used to go with his father to the rehearsals so he nurtured love for the theatre from his childhood. Tendulkar himself considers those rehearsals as a kind of "Magic show". Because like magic he saw the living beings change into characters. He saw with wonder the male performing the roles of woman by changing their voice and movements. He didn't have any exposure to other theatre except what his father staged.

Tendulkar had other **brother** named **Raghunath** and **sister Leela**. His two elder sisters died in infancy. He had two younger brothers but- he was the favourite child of his parents. He was sickly child and suffering from cough and asthmatic wheezing. So special care, protection and love were provided to this sickly boy by the parents for fear of losing him if not protected well. He was given the **pet name "Papia"** and above all he was known as a **"Mother's child"** being favourite of his mother. Emotionally he was more attached with his mother than his father. He remembers how his mother used to feed him forcefully.

Due to his unhealthy body the family servant used to take him to school. It was municipal school. As usual it had small dingy rooms with awful toilets and it had no playground and water at times. In the school also special attention was given to him as he belonged to somewhat well to do family. His teachers used to borrow story books from him and by becoming partial they left him alone at the examination. Thus he studied in an average Indian school, which has no basic facilities but he carries those moments in comparison with sophisticated school where he studied later in life. At 9 years of age he attended "Chikisaha samooha", where he found himself totally strange among the sophisticated children and spacious buildings.

Tendulkar surprisingly started his career as a **writer** at a very early stage of life. He wrote stories and essays when he was **6** years of age. His father was a writer, director and actor so creativity was inborn in him. The unpublished work of his father lay at home and little Tendulkar passed his time with books and had read novel and short stories of eminent writers so he grew up in a literary atmosphere. The seed had already been sown in little mind for literature and gradually it took the shape of huge tree.

He had never imagined himself to be a writer in his childhood. As a small child he wanted to be an engine driver or an acrobat in circus and dreamt of wondering from place to place astonishing the crowd by daredevil acts. He used to visit fairs and circus with his father which were like big fairyland for him. So childlike curiosity, interest and amazement surrounded him along with his keen interest in reading. Sunday and vacation had special attraction for him. On Sunday morning his father used to take him to a large bookshop of his friend used to buy books of his choice. In evening his father took him to chowpatty beach and they travelled in train from Charni Road to Colaba which attracted him a lot. During summer vacation the family used to go for Goa or to Port Ratnagiri.

Tendulkar remembers that his father was a strict disciplinarian, impractical, stubborn but an honest man. "To be honest is a disqualification in todays world" and so Mr. Dhondopant Tendulkar never got the honour of being honest and idealist. He never took bribes or extra fees. But he felt proud to be poor and was very much content with life. Due to this the later life of his father was miserable. The elder brother Raghunath quarrelled with him and left the home. His father was against the dowry system and so Tendulkar's sister Leela didn't get married and had to remain single. It seems that the father had never got family love due to certain principles.

Apart from the influence of the father, Raghunath, his brother also played formative influence on Tendulkar. His brother was a follower of Gandhi and Gandhian principles. He used to attend political congress meetings. The father wanted him to be active in studies but he went astray. He wanted to marry Hansa Wadkar which was unbearable for the idealist father and so the family separated from Raghunath and moved to Kolhapur. Tendulkar used to get gifts like pastries, sweets and pen from his brother. He used to go for English movies with his brother. But his brother died miserably due to alchoholic habit.

The later childhood of Tendulkar passed at Kolhapur – a princely state in Maharastra. At Kolhapur he made himself noticeable by his excellence in reciting English poems. When he was **11 years** old, he **wrote** and **directed** and **acted "Maya Bazaar".** This way, the journey of this veteran writer towards performing arts started. At Kolhapur his friend was the son of one prominent playwright named Na vi kulkarni, who shared the same literary interest with Tendulkar. He even worked as a **child artist** in **two Marathi** Films.

As a teenager, at the **age** of **13** the family shifted to Pune and he attended a new school. He believed that he might have completed matriculation but the **Quit India Movement** was in momentum and Tendulkar was one of those who obeyed Gandhi's call to boycott the school. He started taking part in campaign against Britishers and he used to attend the early morning meetings without informing his parents. At the **age** of **14** while attending such meeting, he **was arrested** and the family came to know about Tendulkar's active participation in freedom fighting. Again he attended the school but now he started bunking the classes and developed the habit of spending the monthly fees of the **school** in watching English films. The visuals had a good impact on him. This exposure to the theatre at an early age has had its strong influence on him as a **successful** dramatist. He says in an interview, "As a school boy I had watched the Hollywood films playing in my hometown, not once, but each one over and over again. I still remember the visuals, not the dialogues which I didn't understand. A more conscious education in what the visual could do came when I worked with the Rangayan Theatre group in Bombay, but watching Marcel Marceau from the last seat in the last row was an enthralling experience. Not a single word was uttered, but so much was expressed. After that I wrote mimes for quite a while. I felt the visual had unlimited possibilities, the word was useless. But I am a playwright, words are my tools, I had to use them." Apart from Films he denoted his time at the city library in reading which helped him a lot during his career as a journalist. But his father was disappointed seeing the poor prospect of Tendulkar.

At Pune, Tendulkar found the **Role Model** of his life – **Dinkar BalKrishna Mokashi,** a radio mechanic but a good writer. He led a very simple life and Tendulkar was impressed by his personality and the informality of his writing style. His other **Role Model** was **Vishnu Vinayak Bokil,** a teacher and a writer. Tendulkar liked his light hearted, jovial and exuberant style. He remembered one incident of the school when Mr. Vinayak asked the students to look at the names of rank holders of the school on the board and asked, "Where are those top rankers now? Does anyone know?"Then he said that the students should pass the exam as the parents pay the fees but the marks they get were not everything. He advised them to develop their personality in other directions also. It worked as a boosting to the teen Tendulkar to look beyond the school. Later on, as a writer Tendulkar dedicated one of his book to this school teacher Mr. Vinayak.

At 16, Tendulkar **left the school** for good. He had no friends and no any communication with his parents. He wanted to talk! But with whom! He had to talk with himself! And he put all his dialogues with his own self on paper through various forms-poems stories, film scripts and at this stage of his life his writing acquired a conscious motivation.

At the age of **22** he wrote his **First full length original play "Grihastha"** which flopped like anything and he took an oath that he would never write a play in life and to his surprise he has written **28 full length** plays as well as he has been **working actively** in the theatre world for the last **45 years.**

He always considers himself a writer first and a playwright after words. About his love for writing he writes,

"The point is more than a playwright, I consider myself to be a writermeaning I loved to indulge in the physical process of writing. I enjoy this process even when there is nothing to be said. Give me a piece of paper any paper and pen and I shall write as naturally as a bird flies or a fish swims. Left to myself, I scribble. And I never get tired of writing… Especially when I write in my mother tongue i.e. Marathi. Writing gives me a pleasure which has no substitute. However, tired I am physically or mentally, the moment I pick up the pen and begin running it on a paperany piece of paper I feel good I feel refreshed I feel as if I am born again. Writing by itself is a luxury for me. When I write, I forget myself, I forget my anxieties…"

He has been writing in different roles by using different mediums. He was **journalist**. He had been **sub-editor** and executive editor in journals and assistant editor of a daily. He used to write editorials with the information received from the second hand sources. This filled him with great dissatisfaction. He says,

"It started with my journalistic dissatisfaction but it grew into much bigger proportions in the sense that it became a matter of conscience as a human being. I became restless."

The violence, the oppression and the exploitation in the society that he witnessed made him restless. And journalism could not offer him a viable solution for his mental agitation. But it does shape his dramatic career. **Gowri Ramnarayan**, therefore points out: "With his exposure to Marathi theatre from childhood, and journalistic background Vijay Tendulkar turned contemporary socio-political situations into explosive drama."

His desire was to start a daily newspaper column and he enjoyed **writing a column** for **six months** in 1993, when Babri Masjid was destroyed. And during those six months he didn't write anything but only enjoyed column writing. He well remembered that during his journalistic days he sometimes wrote for astrology column, when the 'official' astrologer did not reach in time and he enjoyed in forecasting bright future for the unknown readers of the column. As a writer he found good fun in playing the **role** of **an astrologer**.

Being versatile he can put himself in any role. During the period of struggle he did **Ghost writing** with full knowledge that his name would not appear and become known to the readers. He took it as a role with its own "character". His inner personality as a writer underwent a natural change to suit the role. Along with his job in a newspaper he started writing short story and play and even Ghost writing for additional income. His writing developed according to the demands of the roles. He also worked as a **Public Relation Officer** in an industry and wrote copy for add-agencies. He **translated** American Books for the united information services and wrote **scripts** for non-descript Government Documentaries. He played different roles in order to earn his livelihood but his writing practice has brought perfection in writing skill.

Vijay Tendulkar, as a sensitive, sensible and responsible citizen, could not quieten his agitated conscience with his journalistic career. So he left journalism when he received Nehru Fellowship for the 1973-75. During this period, he travelled extensively throughout India and saw directly all kinds of violence. **From this experience, he infers:**

"Unlike communists I don't think that violence can be eliminated in a classless society, or, for that matter, in any society. The spirit of aggression is something that the human being is born with. Not that it's bad. Without violence man would have turned into a vegetable."So he perceived both the positive and negative faces of violence.

Regarding ideology he says,

"I do not align myself to any political ideology.......I do have my sympathies with the left"He does not subscribe to any ideology in his plays. Nor does he write for commercial purpose.

Moreover, in the words of **Mr. Barve,**

"Tendulkar's plays helped to refine Marathi drama that was so far polluted by propaganda for political awakening and social reforms, cheap and vulgar entertainment". Tendulkar does not subscribe to any particular political Ideologies, as they, including Marxism, are unable to understand the complex human situation and to suggest any viable solution to our Hydra-headed problems. Yet he does not lack political awareness.

He says to **Gowri Ramnarayan** in an interview,

"I had a political background, I was involved in the 1942 movement.Journalism developed my political sense, curiosity for instance ....naturally this got in my writing."

He was actively associated with civil liberties movements in Maharashtra. All this shows his great concern for his country and society. He is a realist and refuses to be fooled by romantic concepts of reforms and movements. He exposed the flaws and the inevitable failure of unrealistic reforms and movements in his plays.

Mr. Tendulkar considers himself as an **actor-writer** and himself acted on the stage during his apprentice days in the theatre but did not find it as exciting as writing. He was an actor on the stage of his creative mind. According to him he acts as he writes in his mind he emotes the **lives** of the character as he writes. They are not written words but a total and spontaneous expression of the mind and the personality of the character which includes not only the words but also the eloquent silence in between the words-broken sentences, the subtle emphasis on certain words, even the pitch of the voice, the gestures of the hands. He can 20 visualize the position of the characters on the stage – the total composition of the scene and even the lighting. Thus he acted their speech, behavior patterns and their ways of looking at things. So he believes he can act better than others because he has acted his play out when he wrote the play. **Mr. Tendulkar** was basically **a man of theatre**, which he had inherited from his father and eldest brother. He had a curiosity for this performing art and subconscious and unquenched desire to explore the magic and beauty of this form. His love for the theatre continued as he wrote plays at school, acted in plays, watched it, discussed it and for the last 45 years he was in the world of theatre. He believes that performing art is addictive.

He writes,

"You can learn the "grammar" but art is not mere grammar. It is an expression it provides endless learning by experiments, by committing mistakes."

He remembered that at a very early stage of his life he had developed curiosity for people and consciously noted the speech habits of people, their manners and personal peculiarities. He gives an expression to it in his writing so some of his characters are related to certain living persons. He believed that the creative process is complicated process. The characters would appear in utter chaos till he conceives it. He could never write a play with only idea or theme in mind but he needed character first with him. He writes,

"I could not proceed to write a play unless I saw my characters as real life people, unless I could see them moving doing things by themselves, unless I heard them emoting, talking to each other, I was never able to begin writing my play only with an idea or a theme in mind. I had to have my characters first with me …….." Thus, they are not puppets but living persons of distinction.

About the structuring of his play he said he had never attended any courses for this skill but he had learnt it by trial and error method which is very costly. He wrote that one has to own money in experimental theatre. No one sponsors the play and by the time the players correct the mistakes they are doing the last show of the play. For him, the Rehearsal Hall had become the learning ground. In absence of theatrical devices the inner mechanism of a play with its positive and negative points were laid open and he learnt a lot from these brain- storming rehearsal sessions. Apart from experimenting in the theatre, watching rehearsals he used to see play every day once, twice or thrice in one day. He did not bother whether the play is good or bad but it helped him in internalizing the techniques of playwriting – especially the structuring of the play.

He learnt a lot by watching films because a film also has to have a structure. Even the **concerts** of **classical music impressed** him though he did not know its grammar but classical music has its strict rules and regulations. The **reading** of **the poems** also supplied him the knowledge about compact structure and a form. The visit to the **Art Galleries** made him aware about the rhythm, form and structure in good painting. Apart from all these **Peter Brook's** Book (Master Craftsman in the art of Theatre) taught him the foremost principles of theatre world that all visual art including the art of the theatre, have one thing in common- The space, and it is the skill of the dramatist that how meaningfully and ingeniously he fills the space.

Arundhati Banerjee says,

"Tendulkar's first major work that set him apart from previous generation Marathi playwrights was *Manus Navache Bel (An Island called Man)* (1955). His dramatic genius was cutout for the newly emerging, experimental Marathi theatre of the time. His direct association with Rangayan at this point of his career and continous interaction with such theatre personalities as Vijaya Mehta, Arvind and Sulabha Despande, Kamalakar Sarang Madhav Vatve and Damoo Kenkre provided new impetus for creative faculties. Thus Manus Navache Bel was closely followed by a spate of plays (1958). *Madhlya Bhinti (The walls Between) Chimnicha Ghar Hota Menacha (Nest of wax) (1958) Mee Jinklo Mee Harlo (I won, I lost) (1963) Kavlanchi Shala (school for crows) (1963) and Sari Ga Sari (Rain o Rain) (1964)* which would chart the course of avant-grade Marathi theatre during the next few years. There seems to be a consistency of theme and treatment in them despite the apparently desperate nature of their subjects. In all these early plays, Tendulkar is concerned with the middle class individual set against the backdrop of a hostile society."

Most of Tendulkar's plays are in the naturalistic writing. However, his Ghashiram Kotwal is in the folk tradition while his last two plays *Niyatioya Bailala (To Hell with Destiny)* and *Safar (The Tour)* emplay fantasy. The play **"Silence! The court is in session"** (1967) made him the centre of a general controversy. He has already been called the angry young man of the Marathi theatre. He was considered a rebel against the established values of a fundamentally orthodox society **Encounter in** Umbugland (1974) is a political allegory (1971) **The Vultures** shocked the conservative sections of Marathi people with its naturalistic display of cupidity, sex, and violence. **Sakharam Binder** (1972) is probably Tendulkar's most intensely naturalistic play and shocked the conservative society even more than **The Vultures**. In **Ghashiram Kotwal** (1972) he moves from the naturalistic writing in to the folk tradition, it explains the power game that are found in Indian politics. **Kamala** (1981) is based on **a** real life incident reported in The Indian Express by Ashwin sarin. Kanyadaan is also one of the controversial play and branded as anti – Dalit play. It actually tries to show how our romantic idealism fails.

He wrote his plays in Marathi, First, he influenced Marathi theatre and guided it. Later, his impact extended to other Indian languages as his plays were translated into them. Tendulkar perceived the realities of the human society without any reconceived notions, reacted to them as a sensitive and sensible human being and wrote about them in his plays as a responsible writer. He never wrote to win a prize or an award.

He says,

"I have written about my own experience and about what I have seen in others around me. I have been true to all this and have not cheated my generation. I did not attempt to simplify matters and issues for the audience when presenting my plays, though that would have been easier occupation. Sometimes my plays jolted society out of its stupor and I was punished. I faced this without regrets. It is an old habit with me to do what I am told not to do. My plays could not have been anything else. They contain my perceptions of society and its value and I cannot write what I do not perceive".

In his plays he deals with the issues of gender inequality, social inequality, power games, self alienation, sex and violence. His characters are very much real. They are neither completely good nor completely bad. He liberated Marathi stage from the tyranny of conventional theatre with its mild doses of social and political satire for purpose of pure entertainment.

Mr. M. Sarat Babu writes,

"Vijay Tendulkar portrays the contemporary society and the predicament of man in it with a special focus on the morbidity in his plays, which remind us of Nietzche's words "the disease called man" and also Freud's description of human civilization as "a universal neurosis". His plays touch almost every aspect of human life in the modern world and share the disillusionment of the post modern intellectuals, however they seem to highlight three major issues : gender, power and violence."

Vijay Tendulkar devoted his life for the world of theatre as he says ,

"What I like about those years is that they made me grow as a human being. And theatre which was my major concern has contributed to this in a big way. It helped me to analyse my own life and the lives of others. It led me to make newer and newer discoveries in the vast realm of the human mind which still defies all available theories and logic. It is like an everintriguing puzzle or a jungle which you can always enter but has no way out…"Such a prolific and versatile writer has been felicitated with many awards and honours like

1. The Maharashtra State Government Award (1956, 1969 and 1973)

2. The Sangeet Natak Akademi Award (1971)

3. The Filmfare Award (script writer) (1980,1983)

4. The Padmabhushan (1984)

5. The Saraswati Samman (1993)

6. The Kalidas Samman (1999)

7. The Maharashtra Gaurav Puraskar (1999)

8. The Jansthan Award (1999)

9. Katha Chudamani Award (2001)

This legendary theatre man passed away on **19th May, 2008**. He was suffering from Myasthenia Gravis, a neuromuscular disease. He died at the age of 80 in a private hospital at Pune where he was hospitalized since 10th April, 2008.Shirish Prayag, Director of Prayag Hospital stated,"At the time of his demise he was extremely calm and quiet. There was an expression of contentment on his face. His face did not reflect any pain."

Mr. Prayag stated that the family members had discussed the possibility of eye donation but it was decided that since Tendulkar had not expressed such a wish it would be improper to do so. Tendulkar who was in Pune, since he was last discharged from hospital had refused to go back to Mumbai."

According to his wish his last rites were performed at the Vaikanth electric crematorium and prominent theatre and film personalities including Mohan Agashe, Satish Alekar, Haider Ali, Amruta Subhash, Amol Palekar and Atul Pethe, university of Pune vice-chancellor Narendra Jadhav paid last tribute to Tendulkar at the crematorium.

➤ **Condolence Messages on Vijay Tendulkar's DeathPresident Pratibha Patil** said in her condolence message "Vijay Tendulkar was not only an acknowledged figure in Indian literature but also helped Marathi and all of Indian theatre attain recognition at the international level."

➤ **Prime Minister Manmohan** Singh in a condolence message to Tendulkar's family said, "his strog espousal of women's empowerment and the empowerment of the downtrodden has shaped public consciousness in post independence India."

➤ **Leader of Opposition L K Advani** also paid glowing tributes to Tendulkar. He said the playwright was an outstanding writer who gave Marathi theatre a national and international profile."His place, many of which were translated into Hindi and other Indian Languages, were both creative and carried a strong social message,"

➤ **Maharashtra Chief Minister Vilasrao Deshmukh** also condoled the death of eminent playwright Vijay Tendulkar.In his condolence message, Deshmukh said: "The nation has lost the literary genius and dramatist par excellence. With Tendulkar's death an eventful era has come to an end."

➤ Noted film **director Shyam Benegal** said : "Tendulkar was one of the greatest playwright of Indian theatre in the last 50 years. Tendulkar wrote screenplay of my films "Nishant" and "Manthan". I respected his creativity and admired him as a human being." "He was a senior professional form our field and his contribution to the Indian theatre was immense," Benegal added.

➤ **Film director Govind Nihlani** said : "Tendulkar brought modernity to Marathi theatre. He pioneered a paradigm shift in the vision of looking at society and reflecting it through theatre and cinema."

➤ **Bollywood superstar Mr. Amitabh Bachchan** said : " Vijay Tendulkar was a strong and fearless writer and a great mind. I am deeply saddened to hear the news of his passing away." Amitabh was full of admiration for the man who re-wrote many rules of stage writing. "In today's world it is difficult and though to take a committed stand and pursue it. Vijay Tendulkarji did. And that was his strength. At times this stand is the solitary voice of reason often misunderstood but seldom wrong."

➤ **Amol Palekar said**: "His death is a loss to theatre and literature. wonder whether this losss will ever be recovered. I am glad I could do my share of archiving his entire body of work for the younger generation when my wife Sandhya Gokhale and I organized a Ten Festival in 2006 which went on for a week.

List of Vijay Tendulkar's Works :
One Act :
    Thief Police
    Ratra Ani Itar Ekankika (1957)
    Chitragupta, Aho Chitragupta (1958)
    Ajgar Ani Gandharv (1966)

Bhekad Ani Itar Ekankika (1969)

Ekekacha

Andher Nagari

Collection of Stories :

Kaachpatre (1957)

Dwandwa (1961)

Gane (1966)

Phulpakharu (1970)

Essays :

Kovil Unhe (1971)

Rat Rani (1971)

Phuge Savanache (1974)

Ram Prakar (1994)

Children's Plays :

Ithe Bale Miltat (1960)

Patlachya Poriche Lageen (1965)

Chimna Bandhto Bangla (1966)

Chambhar Chauksiche Natak (1970)

Novels :

Kadambari

Katha Eka Vyathechi : Henry James

Nave Ghar : Nave Ayushya : Grace Jordan

Prempatre : Henry James

Aage Barho : G L Letham (1958)

Gele Te Divas (1958)

Devanchi Manse

Amhu Harnhar Nahi: L E Wilder

Ranphul : S L Arora (1963)

Chityachya Magawar : W W Tiberg

Clarke (1957)

Humour :

Karbhareen : Doroothy Von Doren

Biography :

Dayechi Devta : H D Wiloston

To Aamchayasathi Ladhla (Roosevelt) : K O Pear

Film Script (Marathi)	**Film Script (Hindi)**
Samana	Nishant
Sinhasan	Manthan
Umbartha	Akrosh
Akriet	Ardha Satya
22 June 1897	Aaghat

Play	Original Title	Original Author	Original Language	Institution	Director	First Show	Pub.	Yrs.
Adhe Adhure	Adhe Adhure	Mohan Rakesh	Hindi	Theatre Unit	Satyadev Dube	11th Jan. 1970	Popular	1971
Lincolon Che Akherche Divas	Last Days of Lincolon	Mark Doran	English	-	-	-	Majestic	1964
Lobh Nasava hi Vinanti	Hasty Heart	John Patrick	English	Rangayan	Arvind Deshpande	-	Parchure	-
Tughaluq	Tughaluq	Girish Karnad	Kannda	Avishkar	Arvind Deshpande	17th Aug. 1971	Niklanth	1971
Vasarach Akra	A street Car Named Desire	Tenesse Williams	English	-	-	-	Popular	1966

Dramatic Works

Title	Institute	Director	First Show	Publication
Ghrihasth (The House Holder)	Mumbai marathi Sahitya Sangha, Drama Wing	Damu Kenkare	1955 Exact date not known	-
Sjro,amt (The rich)	Bharatiya vidya bhavan kala kendra	Vijaya Mehta	12th Dec. 1955	1955
Manus navache Bet (An Island Called man)	Lalit kala Kendra	Damu kenkare	28th Oct. 1956	1956
Madhalya Bhinti (Middle Walls)	Best Art Section	Nandkumar Rawate	4th Nov. 1958	1958
Chimanicha Ghar Hota menacha (The Wax House of the Sparrow	Rangmancha	Vijaya Mehta	27th Dec. 1959	1960
Mi Jinkalo (I Won, I lost)	Rangayan	Vijaya Mehta	20th Oct. 1963	1963
Kavlyanchi Shala (School for Crows)	Rangayan	Vijaya Mehta	5th Dec. 1963	1964
Sarga Sari (Drizzle O Drizzle)	Mumbai Marathi Sahitya Sangh, Drama wing	Arvind Deshpande	18th May 1964	1964
Ek Hatti Mulagi (An obstinate Girl)	Kala Vaibhav	Almram Bhende	21th Nov. 1966	1968

Shatata Court Chalu Ahe (Silence! The Court is in Session)	Rangayan	Arivind Deshpande	28th Dec. 1967	1968
Jhala Anant Hanumant	-	Arvind Deshpande	-	1968
Dambdwipacha Mukbala (An Encounter in Umbugland)	Rangayan	Arvind Deshpande	10th Dec. 1969	1974
Gidhade (The Vulture)	Theatre Unit	Shriram lagu	29th May 1970	1971
Ashi Pakhare Yeti (So Come Birds)	Progressive Dramatic Association, Pune	Jabbar Patel	26th Nov. 1970	1970
Sakharam Binder	Welcome theatres	Kamalar Sarang	10th mar. 1972	1972
Bhalya kaka	Natya Mandar	Arvind Deshpande	5th April 1972	1974
Gharate Amuche Chan (Nice is our Nest)	Welcome Theatre	kamalakar Sarang	28th Oct. 1972	1973
Ghashiram Kotwal	Progressive Dramatic Association, Pune	Jabbar Patel	16th Dec. 1972	1973
Baby	nateshwar	Kamalakar Sarang	29th Aug. 1976	1975
Bhai Murarrao	Theatre Academy Pune	Mohan gokhale	13th Sept. 1977	1975

Pahije Jatiche	-	Arvind Deshpande	-	1976
Mitrachi Goshta (A Friend's Story)	Bhumika	Vinay Aapte	15th Aug. 1981	1982
kamala	Kala Rang	kamalakar Sarang	7th Aug. 1981	1982
Kanyadan	INT	Sadashiv Amarapurkar	12th Feb. 1983	1983
Vithala	INT	Sadashiv Amarapurkar	22nd May 1985	1985
Chiranjeev Saubhagya kanshini	Abhishek	Kamalakar Sarang	14th Dec. 1991	-
Safar	Avishkar	Sulbha Deshpande	6th Jan. 1992	-
Niyatichya bailala Ho (To Hell with the Bull of the Fate)	-	-	-	-

2. SAKHARAM BINDER : AN OVERVIEW

Geeta kumar in **"Portrayal of women in Tendulkar's Sakharam Binder and Shantata! Court Chalu he"** writes

"Sakharam Binder" is probably Tendulkar's most intensely naturalistic play. "It created dramatic history by challenging the Censor Board because it was initially banned. Tendulkar's depiction of a character who rejects the artificial values imposed by the society and the use of extremely vulgar and outspoken language incensed the Censor authorities."

Mr. V. M. Madge also opines the same **in "Sakharam Binder: An Unwitting Deconstruction."**

"Sakharam Binder was staged first on 10th March 1972. Following "The Vultures" (1970) which had ruffled middle-class sensibilities a bit, the play confirmed Tendulkar's image as a radical and iconoclastic dramatist. There was quite a storm with regard to the raciness of dialogue, the 'bold' portrayals of characters like Sakharam and Champa, and especially Sakharam's lashing out against the hypocrisy of people. Almost thirty five years later, what strikes one about the play is not so much the boldness of theme and character as the inner contradictions of the central character and the thematic confusion."

Sakharam, a book-binder was a brahmin but rejects all the 'code of conduct' of that caste and lives his life according to his own desires. Mr. Tendulkar points out in his article "Muslim and I" that Sakharam is unmarried male, unmarried parlty because of his meager income as a book-binder in a printing press and also because of his complex personality which is basically of a loner. He is a man who has always lived outside the established norms of decent society and has learned to challenge them in words as well as in action. He needs a woman in his house for sex as well as for taking care of the household chores. For this he picks up a married woman who is in the dumps, who has been driven out by her husband- lock, stock and barrel. He takes her home to live with him till one of the two decides to end the "contract" and calls it quits. In his relationships he observes a code of conduct and insists that it should be observed by the women till they cohabit. He makes his code of conduct known to every new woman he brings home before she formally makes her decision to stay.

Tendulkar's characters always come from real life and he has heard about such a man like Sakharam from his friend and with the use of his dramatic art he made him alive on the stage. He focuses on the several issues of human life, nature and the society in the play. They are

1) Manifestation of violence in Human being.
2) Manifestation of physical lust in Human being.
3) Exploration of Marriage institute v/s Live – in – Relationship

The play title stands for Sakharam who is a loner, bereft of familial ties, and whose profession as a book-binder enables him to cock a snook at the conservative society milieu and live a bizarre life on his own terms. It was written by Vijay Tendulkar in 1972 and banned in 1974 for its outrageous narrative.

3. MANIFESTATION OF VIOLENCE IN HUMAN BEING

Sakharam Binder, Ghashiram Kotwal, Silence! The court is in session which made Tendulkar a popular playwright, are experiments of an intense and deeper impulse and not just a matter of superficial innovation. A kind of new freedom and conviction are seen in these plays. The phrase "sex and violence" is very loosely attributed to, in the discussion of these plays. But in none of these the theme of sex and violence is superficial as it forms an important part of the content of the plays. The theme of violence pervades quite blatantly in most of his plays. Tendulkar was influenced by Artaud's idea of relating the theme of anguish to the theme of violence.

When he was awarded a fellowship by Nehru Memorial Fund committee Tendulkar elaborated the theory of violence in his project "Emerging pattern of violence," Structuring his theory on the concept of the theatre of cruelty. He does not consider the occurrence of human violence as something loathsome or ugly as it is innate in human nature.

Ever since he wrote Silence the court is in session. Tendulkar has discovered that violence makes man fascinating and there are many variations in the way violence manifests itself in the way man expresses it. Its various manifestations and how they are moulded by each person are important for a study of human nature. He believes that violence is a basic quality, when this understanding of human nature is translated into a play it not only becomes an explosive piece of art but also a thesis. Tendulkar unabashedly presents and defends it, According to him the most important point is to keep the violence raw while depicting it on stage, not to dress it up with any fancy trapping and not to make it palatable. In Sakharam Binder he tries to present this innate human nature of violence without any decoration. Here he presents a raw chunk of life with all its ugliness and cruelty which was more than a shock to refined and prudish middle class audience.

In the opening of the play, the very first speech of Sakharam indicates the innate violent nature of him as he says –

1. "When I lose my temper, I beat the life out of people"

This violent nature of Sakharam appears in the Act I , scene VI, when on Ganesh Chathurthi Laxmi does not allow Dawood his friend, to participate in the puja because he is muslim. Sakharam beats Laxmi with belt. Sakharam's violent nature is accompanied with too much physical lust. Physically Laxmi appears to him "Frigid" and at night he tries to excite her by asking her to laugh compulsorily, which she cannot and he threatens –

2. "No, you can sleep later. Get up and laugh. Laugh or I'll choke the life out of you. Laugh! Laugh!"

Even when he beats her he says –

3. "Laugh this minute, or I'll twist your arm. I will. I'll get the belt."

So he satisfies his whimsical desires by beating his wife. The beating of his wife also satisfies his ego, that being the master of the house he can rule the house. His violent nature is very well reflected when Laxmi makes a revolt against him, speaking bluntly to him –

4. "I've never heard a kind word here. Always barking, orders, curses, oaths. Threatening to throw me out: kicks and blows there I was in agony after I'd been belted and all you wanted me to do was laugh. Laugh and Laugh again.........If I die I'll be free of this once and for all."

When Laxmi is fed up with Sakharam's violence, she decides to separate herself from him. But again her misfortune brings her back to Sakharam's house. He is not ready to allow her again in the house. He has not forgotten the insulting words of Laxmi which she showered on him while leaving him. Remembering that insult, he again beats Laxmi mercilessly. If

Champa, his new wife had not interfered, he would have murdered Laxmi.

The extreme point of his violent nature is shown when in a fit of anger, he murders Champa, his new wife, who is keeping physical relations with his friend Dawood. Being a member of low income group of the society, beating, abusing, have become a part of Sakharam's personality. He considers himself as the "master" of the house and he establishes his authority by beating his wife.

Tendulkar believes that just as good and evil co-exist in one's self, in the same manner love and violence, these two emotions are part of one's self. The trait of violence is very much present in everyone, only its proportion differs from one person to another. Sakharam makes a show of his violent nature by giving threat, abusing and beating his wife. But Tendulkar tries to present subtle violence in Laxmi's character. Outwardly she appears to perform the role of devoted, ideal wife, who obeys each command of Sakharam. But at the end of the play she exhibits the innate violence of her personality. Sakharam becomes confused after killing Champa, but Laxmi soothes him. For her it is not a murder but Sakharam has killed a sinner. Laxmi who appears throughout the play as an embodiment of virtues, observer of morality, does not find Sakharam's act as a crime. In fact, it is she who excites him to murder her. The dead body of Champa does not terrify her, instead she herself starts digging up the grave for Champa and suggests to him to bury her. Sakharam who has been appearing very violent and bold became terrified and Laxmi tries to console him by saying.

"She was unfaithful to you. You are a good man. God will forgive you." So, if we peep into the psyche of Laxmi, she also appears violent just like Sakharam.

Even the character of Champa also exhibits the trait of violence. She is similar to Sakharam. Like him she also drinks, uses abuses and beats her husband Fozdar Sinde. By beating him, insulting him Champa shows her contempt for him. So through the depiction of such characters and their nature, Tendulkar demonstrates the basic and essential complexity of human nature which is neither black nor white but varying shades of grey.

4. MANIFESTATION OF PHYSICAL LUST IN HUMAN BEING

After writing **Gidhade** Tendulkar commented that he did not think that he could write such a play wrought with violence and sex, again. But he did. Just sixteen months later he wrote **Sakharam Binder**. In the words of a critic, commenting on the play soon after it was produced :

"For many decades no play has created such a sensation in the theatre world of Maharashtra as Vijay Tendulkar's **Sakharam Binder**.

It evoked even more resistance from the censor boards than Gidhade had. The use of extremely vulgar language and exhibition of sex incensed the censor authorities. The play contains five bed-room scenes

[Act I, - scene-V, VIII

Act II – scene – III, V

Act III – scene – V]

Tendulkar's philosophy of life includes Man, his body and soul. While depicting the man-woman relationship he shows something uncommon and strange, but it is equally true that he never gives a perverted and vulgar form to this depiction. In this play Sakharam, the main character comes from the lower strata of the society, who does not observe any moral code of conduct. He rejects the institution of marriage, but he needs a woman for his physical needs. So on a contractual basis he brings home different women who are abandoned by their husbands.

Laxmi, the woman, whom he brings in the opening of drama fits into the socially approved mould of a good woman and a good wife. She is deserted by her husband because she has not borne her husband a child. She is hard working, willing to take her husband's beating and to submit to his cruel demands in bed. Sakharam makes clear to her in the very first speech along with other commands, his expectations from Laxmi as a wife. He says –

"And one last thing…….. you'll have to be a wife to me. Anyone with a little sense will know what to make of that."

Sakharam, as a man, wants Laxmi's involvement in bed-room. But she is unable to satisfy him. Sakharam finds her laughing and giggling with ant. He wants the same kind of Laxmi at night but she cannot involve herself. So Sakharam has to compel her to laugh at night in order to enjoy her. He feels excited only when she laughs. Even when she is beaten, he needs to hear Laxmi's laughter. It gives him courage to take his sexual rights from her. He says,

"You laugh for the ant. But you won't laugh when I ask you to. I'll twist that foot of yours, you get me? Now sit up, you're not to sleep. Wake up."

So, Laxmi appears to him somewhat "frigid" to his physical demands as she cannot participate freely in sex. With the coming of Champa, the second woman Shakharam is able to fulfill his sexuality. He transforms into a sensuous, lewd drunkard with thoughts of only sexual enjoyment. Champa looks seductive, she is the one who has suffered most on account of her voluptuous body. She has abandoned her lecherous but impotent husband. Champa is a sexual challenge to Sakharam. He is lured by her body. While speaking about the rules of the house, he controls a lot to free himself from the lure of her body. Her first response to his physical demand is –

"What is it? Who's that? It's you! Something on your mind again! I told you, didn't I? why won't you understand? If I feel cut up, I can turn nasty. Take care not to rub me the wrong way. I don't like it – all that man-woman staff."

But soon she submits to him with enough liquor. Initially Sakharam is totally lost in her sensuous body. He just cannot concentrate on his work and used to come early from work as soon as he remembers his fun at night. He brings liquor at noon and excites Champa who is not at all prepared for it at such an unusual time. But the liquor makes her weak and she submits to Sakharam. Sakharam even stops going to press and Dawood persuades him to do his job regularly. But Sakharam says –

"I grew up like a cactus – out in the open. I don't scare easy. From now on it is going to be Champa, Champa and nothing more......" Nobody can match her little finger. You don't know what fun Champa is."

But the re-appearance of Laxmi in his life and house changes all. The presence of Laxmi makes him impotent. The presence of Laxmi and Champa in the house has a strange effect on Sakharam as if the two different strands in his character come into direct confrontation creating a psychological turmoil in him and resulting in his temporary impotence. Champa scolds him regarding this –

"Yeah. Can't take it any more- not even with all that drink inside me. If you can't make it go and lie down quiety. Haven't been able to make it this last two days. A sound from the kitchen and you go cold. That's true or not?"

Champa reminds him about his failure in sex due to Laxmi. Which is a big insult of Sakharam. She says –

"Stop that 'Champa-Champa – ' you're not a man – not since she came. She's made an impotent ninny of you. Don't have the guts to take me before her. You turn into a corpse – a worm."

Sakharam realised the reason. All this is happening because of Laxmi's presence. He comes out of his room and tells her –

"Leave this house. This very minute. She says you have made a ninny out of me. You beggar."

Out of rage, he virtually kicks her out of the house for good. A desperate Laxmi plays her trump card. Half terrorised by a ferocious Sakharam, she blurts out what she "saw" the other day, Champa sleeping with Dawood – "It's true – it's the truth – these lips have never spoken a lie yet – she's unfaithful to you – yes – with Dawood. She goes to him – every afternoon – when you're at the press. I've seen them – seen them with my own eyes."

Sakharam's masculinity is doubly hurt through the knowledge of Champa's physical association with Dawood. Since he himself can no longer satisfy her. Hence in his rage he kills Champa.

The portrayal of Champa's character manifests sensuality of woman. She seems to be a nymphomaniac. She declares that her husband Fauzdas Shinde was a lecherous man. She says ,

"He brought me from my mother even before I'd become a woman. He married me when I didn't even know what marriage meant. He'd torture me at night. He branded me, and stuck needles into me and made me do awful, filthy things..."

And she sounds contradictory when she deserts him for his impotency. She considers him as "Corpse." She vehemently declares that she does not like that "man-woman" stuff. Yet her own lust leads her to develop sexual relations with Dawood. She gives up Sakharam because Laxmi's presence make him impotent like her own husband. She has been seeking a man who can satisfy her sexually. And she looks at Dawood who is smitten by her at the very first meeting. Champa, soon after her arrival at Sakharam's house seizes Dawood in her attraction. She boldly changes her clothes before him and excites him to advance in relations. In the presence of Sakharam, she admires Dawood and says –

"He's nice"

Sakharam also realises the situation and tells Dawood –

"Dawood, from now on I'll come to your shop, we'll meet there. That'll be better. What?"

Dawood's response to Champa is not respectful as a person. He just uses the word's like "Wow"! "Terr-i-fic!" for her. He never calls her "Bhabhi" she remains a sensuous woman for him. Champa gives up Sakharam, but her action raises a question – if he becomes impotent only after Laxmi's return, what was he like earlier? Champa hasn't given herself a chance to discover for she has chosen to get totally drunk and not be conscious of him at all.

Through such delineation of characters, Tendulkar explores the manifestation of physical lust in human being.

5. COMPLEXITY OF HUMAN MIND

Though Tendulkar focuses on the middle-class and its suffocations, his chief targets are the human mind, the way of life and the complexities therein. He does not crave for outdated ideals or impossible aims. He is drawn towards "the real", with all its limitations. He mostly exhibits men trying to live independently as human beings drifting along the current of the inevitable. The individual identity of man and his social existence, the harmony and disharmony between the two – these form the essence of Tendulkar's thinking. It can be observed that Tendulkar's plays tend towards existentialism.

Tendulkar seems to present the essential complexity of human nature. So in this play all his characters are a combination of good and evil, weakness and strength. Sakharam, is frank and outspoken and he tries to work out an independent philosophy of life, with no sense of false obligations. He has no social taboos. He drinks heavily, has no sense of guilt and admits to all his vices. Sakharam is a bitter critic of the institution of marriage and attacks husbands while pitying wives. He arranges contractual marriage based on convenience with single women who have been deserted by their husbands. Sakharam, though apparently crude, aggressive and violent, has his own laws of personal morality. The openness of his personality becomes in itself a criticism of the hypocrisy of the middle class. Sakharam ridicules the double standards of the middle class. He flaunts his virility as a make-believe to compensate for his inner weakness and loneliness.

The opening of the play presents him bringing a woman at home to live with her without observing the ritual of marriage. His conversation with the woman, Laxmi, indicates that even in the past he had entertained some such women without marriage. But later on he kicked out them when he realized that he cannot pull on with them any longer. The striking element to be noticed in Laxmi's arrival to his place is that neither Laxmi nor Sakharam is ashamed of, or afraid of living together without getting united into the social sanction of marriage. Of course, they are laughed at by small children for whom it is very strange to see different women coming to sakharam's place and staying there for some time. But they ignore the laughing.

In fact, Sakharam's way of life and his living with different women involves in it the social issue of personal freedom and decency. It is very difficult for any person to maintain an ideal balance between the two. If a person cares for personal freedom social decency suffers. One has to curtail one's own desire for personal freedom in order to observe social norms and decency. Sakharam in this play cannot opt it because he gives more importance to his personal freedom ignoring social decency.

In the case of Laxmi, it becomes much more crucial because she has to sacrifice her respect just for a roof. Whatever she does is not as a champion of personal freedom or as a feminist activist. She does it as a helpless, roofless woman who considers the shelter of house more important than the shelter of respect. Laxmi as a helpless woman accepts to live in Sakharam's house but ironically that shelter cannot offer any safety to her.

The complete reading of the play suggests that the relationship between man and woman in any other form cannot be so much safe, prestigious and treated with honour as the relationship by the way of marriage. Laxmi's idea about safety and shelter is very soon shattered when she is kicked out by Sakharam. Laxmi's going away and Champa's arrival demands a great thought in the play.

Sakharam assures every womon he brings home of his "good" treatment. He frames certain rules for his woman companions. So, Sakharam, in his passionate rejection of the traditional and moral values, tends to contradict himself in word and deed in the absence of well-considered moral alternatives. Though Sakharam keeps on repeating time and again in the play that he is no husband to forget common decency, he wants that the woman who, lives with him shall have to be a wife to him so, while he poses to be a savior, he presents the picture of a brutal perpetrator and wretched victim of all that is bad in society regarding the man woman relationship.

Mr. N. S. Dharan writes in his article **"Sakharam Binder the Impotent fury of a Male Masochist."**

"Sakharam Binder is aggressive in his manners. He projects his ego in order to escape from his super-ego. He always talks of himself as a self made man who has no respect even for gods. In his own words "This Sakharam Binder – he is a terror – He's not scared of God or of God's father. On seeing Laxmi looking for framed gods he says.

"We're not saints. We're men. I tell you worship and prayer can't satisfy the itch. If you want a thing well, you've got to have it......"

All this crude atheistic outbursts of Sakharam Binder, and his own reference to himself as a " terror " stand in sharp contrast to what he tells the terrorised Laxmi a little while later, "I know I'm foulmouthed. Bothers you, doesn't it, even to hear me talk I've been like this right from birth/ born naked my mother used to say. The brat's shameless. He's Mahar born in a Brahmin house."

Tendulkar indicates here that we are living our life in the times when compromise, adjustment, altitude of let go, pulling on, forget and forgive have lost their significance. The sense of individualism has become so much powerful that no body is ready to pull on with anybody. Human relationship has become transitory utilitarian matter in which the principle of " use and throw " is practiced Laxmi's going away and Champs's arrival are the best examples of it.

The playwright fully presents first Sakharam's stay with Laxmi and then his stay with Champa. Both the relationships are lacking in one element which is the foundation of relationship between man and woman faithfulness. Laxmi wanted to remain faithful to Sakharam but Sakharam fails to be faithful to her. And his unfaithfullness to Laxmi is responded to him by Champa's faithfullness to him. It shows one more drawback of Live-in relationship.

Laxmi, appears in the play as the embodiment of the ideal Indian woman, — loyal, docile, hard working, tender-hearted. She is thrown out because she is unable to give birth to a child. Laxmi secretly regards Sakharam as her husband, because she cannot see herself in the kind of unsanctified union he proposes. She therefore wears a mangalsutra in his name, carefully hidden inside her blouse. When she returns to his house after her nephew has thrown her out, she falls at Sakharam's feet and won't let go despite his merciless beating and kicking. Her place is at his feet. She cries.

He is her husband, master, god, with sanction to do what he pleases to with her without fear of retaliation.

There are ironies in Laxmi's character which are subtly pointed out by Tendulkar. She talks to ants and birds, suggesting she is a person of immense compassion for all living things. But her acceptance of the rich variety of created life does not extend to diversity in human beings. She would like to recreate her immediate world in her own image. She reforms Sakharam from the renegade he is into a more or less enthusiastic believer in her god and her ways of worship. He is standing on the very edge between his erstwhile world and hers, when he installs Lord Ganesha, in his home for the first time for the Ganesh festival. But she notices Dawood, Sakharam's closet friend, joining in the worship of the deity and makes a sigh to him not to do so. He may not sing the praises of her god because he is muslim. She is beaten but she will not retract from her position. She has the strength of the martyr, righteously defending the faith as she sees it. Such a woman turns out to be wily and vicious when her survival is threatened by the presence of Champa. She develops an asexual friendship with the other weakling in the play, shinde. Though Laxmi finds nothing wrong with her own association with Shinde, her moral sense is outraged by Champa's affair with Dawood and she uses this opportunity to malign her rival. This brings out the latent hatred in Laxmi for Champa. After Champa's murder she shows greater ruthlessness and presence of mind in covering it up than Sakharam, who is totally bewildered by what he has done.

Champa's character too, offers complexity of human mind. Champa appears as unconventional and strong woman, who has left her husband. She does not behave as a destitute dependent. Here is a woman who will not let a man use her body simply because he is her husband or her patron. If Laxmi draws her strength from being unconventional, Champa draws it from being an independent, self-respecting individual. She possesses contradictory nature. At one stage she says –

"Don't upset me. I don't like that sort of thing......all that man-woman stuff"

Yet she appears as lusty woman. Relating her own life she mentions that she was taken away by a Fauzdar Shinde before her becoming a woman and she finds him impotent in her later life so she deserts him. Both these appear contradictory. Her relationship with Dawood after coming to the place of Sakharam indicates that it may not be Shinde's impotence but her excessive lust must be responsible for the collapse of her married life with Shinde. Her way of life gives an impression to the spectators \readers that she may be a nymphomaniac woman, a woman who is fond of changing her bed partners.

The second arrival of Laxmi in the play offers a greater significance to all these characters. It does not stand for a lone triangle but it gives an idea about the complexity of human relationship, in modern times. Champa shows strange kindness and generosity when she convinces Sakharam to give shelter to Laxmi. Champa does not visualize any possibility of competition from her for she is confident of her own sexual attraction. She pities this homeless, shelterless woman. It is the kindness of this otherwise hard-hearted woman that makes it possible for Laxmi to stay in Sakharam's house.

Yet, it is not only the kindness but greater selfish motive hidden behind Champa's readiness to allow Laxmi to live in the same house. It is possible that she has not true concern for Laxmi. She wants her domestic household responsibilities to be shouldered by Laxmi and in the return of which she would get food and roof. She convinces Sakharam by saying – "Why're you so bothered? She can help me in the house. Anyway I can't cope with the house and with you. She'll look after house. We don't have to give anything except a little food and my old saris."

This shows her selfish motive and drive behind keeping Laxmi in the house. It will also help Champa to go to Dawood for her physical lust. If Laxmi is present only then she can leave the house. There is also a touch of contempt in Champa's treatment of Laxmi, the contempt that a stronger person feels for a weakling.

Catherine Thankamma writes in **"Women that patriarchy created : The plays of Vijay Tendulkar, Mahesh Dattani and Mahasweta Devi'.** "Laxmi is thrown out of her house by her husband but she still considers him her God. Champa on the other hand is a figure of revolt. She hates her husband for the physical and sexual torture he inflicted on her so when he follows her to Sakharam's house she abuses him and kicks him out. Laxmi who accepts and upholds the patriarchal value system hates Champa for ill-treating her husband and sees her death as a kind of divine retribution. Such blind belief in an oppressive system appears even more stifling than Champa's gross vulgarity. Laxmi and Champa thus represent the two polarities of feminine response to patriarchy. Laxmi's response is significant because it is a pointer to the fact that all transgression from the male ordained norms are taboo . Sakharam flaunts his unconventional way of life and his physicality. Yet he is shocked by Champa's violence towards her husband because the use of violence and foul language is the male's prerogative. The fact that it was the physical violence inflicted by her husband that has turned Champa into a creature who has to be driven senseless through liquor before she can submit to sex is of no account. A woman should be the epitome of tolerance and patience.

The minor character Dawood is also a complex character. He does not appear as an ideal friend from the point of view of his relationship with Champa. He is a regular visitor and companion to Sakharam who knows more about Sakharam than Sakharam's knowledge about himself. He stands by Sakharam in his crisis. Tendulkar in his article **"Muslim and I"** writes

"Dawood is a local poor Muslim who earns his living doing odd jobs and is a bachelor. Dawood is a frequent visitor to Sakharam's house and is familiar with Sakharam's non-conformist, odd and colourful life-style. Seeing a new female – a haggard and emaciated one mostly – in Sakharam's house every often comes as no surprise to him. Both are smoking chillum as is their routine at the end of the day. Sakharam dryly and casually describes the plight of Laxmi after she was thrown out by her husband. That Laxmi can hear what he is being told makes Dawood self-conscious and he gestures to Sakharam to stop. But he goes on. The

difference between the sensibility of Sakharam and Dawood, as expressed here is significant. Dawood is shown as more "human" and caring, more circumspect in such respect than his rebel Hindu Brahmin friend Sakharam."

But the arrival of Champa makes him to go astray. He can not restrain her charm and forgets his long cherished friendship with Sakharam. Driven by his fancy for Champa, he comes frequently to Sakharam's house. But suddenly he stops coming. He crosses the limits and develops physical relations with Champa. This very depiction of his personality proves that sometimes physical lust conquers over the pious bond like friendship and

love.

Mr. N.S. Dharan states in **"Sakharam Binder : The impotent Fury of a Male masochist".**

"Sakharam falls because of his "appetite", to satisfy which he goes to any extreme. His ill-treatment of Laxmi, and his helpless slavery to Champa are proofs of this fact. Inwardly, he is a coward. Though he condemns gods for his hard life, he has innate faith in them. He tries to cover up his cowardice, helplessness and above all, his loneliness behind a mask of aggressive boastfulness and animal behaviour. Yet he is aware of his need for reclamation which occurs in the last Act."

Indeed, the depiction of such complexity of human mind, makes Tendulkar's drama very much realistic based on existentialism. **So Chandrashekhar Barve** in his article **"Vijay Tendulkar : The Man who explores the Depths of Life"** writes –

"The existentialist tendencies are openly manifest in Sakharam Binder."

Sakharam's ego tries to manifest itself in a challenging way. It is not ready to be tied down to anything. The influence of Laxmi triggers an inner conflict between the existential ego and the metaphysical I. In effect we see that Sakharam, who has lost his self, has become pitiable because of his spinelessness very much like a string without a kite. When he realizes that he is losing himself, he goes astray, he is frightened and finally his living corpse gets pacified after lifeless and senseless activities.

Sakharam is unpolished and hence the play "Sakharam Binder" appears to be rough. Nevertheless, the play does make its appearance with existentialist traits. To sum up, Tendulkar was the pioneer who changed not only the external framework of Marathi drama but also the limits of the picture of life at the core."

6. EXPLORATION OF MARRIAGE INSTITUTION VERSUS THE CONCEPT OF LIVE-IN-RELATIONSHIP

The institution of Marriage is the foremost Pillar of the society. Man and woman live under the same roof through this institution of marriage. In India, it is impossible to imagine man and woman living together without marriage. This play presents such a situation in which two persons live together in the same house not for "LOVE" but for their own needs with certain agreements. This situation can be compared with the modern trend

known as Live-in-relationship.

Mr. V. B. Despande writes in **"Tendulkar's contribution to Indian Drama"**

"Tendulkar had to fight a courtroom battle in respect of Sakharam Binder. The main objection in this litigation was that the institution of marriage will come into jeopardy because of this play. Of course, nothing of the sort has happened. It is useful to remember in this context that the influence literature wields on society is always minimal as compared to that of technology. The growth and development of a society are slow processes and they cannot be hastened or retarded by one play or novel. Secondly, if the institution of marriage which has been there for centuries or a value system which has sustained a society for ages is going to be destroyed by one single work of art it becomes imperative that we take a second look at the institution or the system. Thirdly, when such charges are made against a talented writer like Tendulkar, ironically enough these very charges in a sense compliment the writer..."

Tendulkar was foresighted man and he presented such a concept of living together without marriage in 1972. Through this play he tries to explore the traditional institute of marriage as well as the drawbacks of "Live-in- Relationship." Here Sakharam, the protagonist is a book-binder who does not believe in the institution of marriage and arranges contractual cohabitation based on convenience with woman who is thrown out by her husband. He is Brahmin but he rebels against the established norms of the society. Due to this, he is rejected by society and lives life of an outcaste. He even visits the prostitutes. But if all his needs had been fulfilled by them he would not have brought any woman at home.

He needs a woman who can look after his home and his daily necessities. But for that he does not like any bondages. He cannot love any woman so he has found out this new concept of living with a woman. So Tendulkar tries to present an attempt made by a man and a woman to live together without marriage under certain agreements against the society. The playwright tries to explore whether it is possible and works out in comparison with the so called institute of marriage.

Sakharam's cohabitation with a woman depends on his rules and he makes it clear as soon as he brings her home. The play opens with such rules of Sakharam for the new woman called Laxmi. He says –

"Come in. Have a good look around. You're going to live here now. This house is like me. I won't have you complaining later on. If you think it's all right, put down your bundle and stay. Otherwise you can clear out...... May be I'm a rascal, a womanizer, a pauper. Why May be? I am all that. And I drink. But I must be respected in my own house. I am the master here. You agree to all this?"

So, the woman has to obey his "code of conduct". Generally the woman has no other option but to obey him.

Laxmi, follows Sakharam like a sheep following the shepherd. She is deserted by her husband because she is unable to give birth to a child. She is helpless as she does not have any relative. The second woman Champa, deserts her husband because he is impotent. She comes to Sakharam, because she fears that if she lives alone her condition would be like prostitute. So the woman who decides to live with Sakharam is helpless. They are in such a critical state of life where they need a man for their protection and a home to live in. Their condition is so miserable that they just overlook the status of man, his house and even the kind of relation they establish with him. They just want a man and house and for that they are ready to compromise with anything.

Through such condition of women like Laxmi and Champa Tendulkar satirizes the institution of marriage which does not grant any security or safety to women. For any reason if the marriage breaks, the woman becomes helpless like Laxmi, unless the man like Sakharam takes her away. Though Sakharam behaves with his woman as a traditional husband – the commander and the master of the house, in his new concept of living with woman, she gets the freedom to desert him if she gets bored by him or his rules and regulations. Though he appears as a dominating man , he allows a woman freedom to leave him. He provides "space" to woman. He seems honest when he justifies his method of living. He says –

"It's good thing I'm not a husband. Things are fine the way they are. You get everything you want and you're not tied down. If you've had enough, if she's had enough you can always part. The game is over. Nothing to bother you after that while it lasts, she has a roof over her head and you get home cooked food. That's a cheap way of fixing all your appetites. And on top of it, the woman stays docile, she works well, she behaves herself. She knows that one wrong move and out she goes."

This new concept of Sakharam satisfies all his needs – physical as well as domestic. Sakharam points out restrained life of married couple. He says –

"It's only when a woman gets married that she goes wrong. She begins to feel, "Now I've got my man! But the husband is proper swine! He ties her down, he doesn't get tied down himself! He flits around again – a free bird."

Sakharam belongs to lower strata and may be uneducated but he holds certain new ideas. He does not like that a woman should regard her husband as a God. He asks Laxmi about her husband's name but being traditional she denies to speak and he says –

"The whole lot of you! All alike where this one thing's concerned. Mention your husband's name and your eyes begins to brim over with tears. He kicks you out of the house, he is out to sequeeze the life out of you. But he's your God. You ought to worship a god like that with shoes and slippers. He should be whipped in public."

Thus, he holds new radical ideas regarding the life of woman. He thinks that a husband is a man only and he should never be regarded as a God by a woman. Laxmi being too orthodox respects him as a god but he becomes angry as he knows that he is man with bundle of weaknesses.

He is against the institution of marriage and hates the authority, enjoyed by the husbands in the society on the name of marriage. There are certain instances in the play which show him as a liberal minded husband who is ready to help his woman in need, or showing concern for her. For example soon after the arrival in the house, when Laxmi is looking for the match box with confusion, he says –

"You must always ask for what you want".

Even he shows her the necessary things, that he has put when Laxmi prepares tea for him, he says –

"Have some yourself. You must take what you want. Mustn't wait to be told".

He is not a traditional looking husband who wants a wife to eat and drink after he himself finishes his own. Even he gives freedom to prepare the meal of her own choice. He never compels her to eat the things which he himself likes to eat whereas generally in the society it happens that a husband wants that the wife should prepare the meal of his choice – but Sakharam says –

"If you're used to rice look around, - you'll find some in the house. There must be some dal too. I don't eat rice."

Even at one stage he offers tea to Laxmi from his own cup which sounds very much untraditional. Though he sounds very much traditional husband when he lists out the rules to be followed by his partner, on certain occasions, his behaviour towards his partner appears very untraditional. He is not only a man of ideas but does put his new ideas regarding freedom and equality of woman into practice. He laughs at woman's blind devotion for the husband. He remembers the former woman who died in the hospital. She was also deserted by her husband and Sakharam brought her home and gave shelter. But on the last moments of her death-bed she spoke husband's name. Sakharam gave her last sip of water, but the name on her lips was her husband's. Laxmi wonders at such a new thinking of Sakharam. Sakharam wants Laxmi to feel free with him and behave with him as a friend but Laxmi who has an image of traditional husband in her mind can not co-operate with him and tries to keep distance from him.

Sakharam even appears as secular man though he is a Brahmin. He is a close friend to Dawood, a muslim and allows him to do Ganesh puja against the will of Laxmi. For him Dawood is a creation of God just like him.

The new woman Champa whom he brings after Laxmi's departure, on certain level matches Sakharam. Laxmi was traditional whereas Champa holds free thinking. She does not behave as a poor dependent. She drinks like Sakharam. Instead of submitting to Sakharam, she gives him the order. On the first day she casually asks him to organize some food. She tries to be independent and self-respecting individual and may be Sakharam likes her for these very qualities of her personality besides her sensuousness. She never regards Sakharam as her god or saviour like Laxmi.

Through Sakharam's life with two women – Laxmi and Champa on certain agreement - , Tendulkar tries to explore the relationship between man and woman or the foundation of their relation through new concept against the so called institution of marriage.

Maya Pandit in **"Representation of family in Modern Marathi plays : Tendulkar, Dalvi and Elkunchwar"** comments on Sakharam Binder thus –

"Sakharam Binder was yet another play in which Tendulkar revealed the political meaning of the institution of family. Though Sakharam proclaimed that his house represents an alternative to marriage, actually the system is just like marriage shorn of all the romantic trappings. It is interesting to note in this context that the Censor Board had refused to issue the play a certificate on the ground that it lowered the sacredness of the institution of marriage that it aroused the passion of dogs and pigs and even that it showed a Hindu wife who assaulted her husband in spite of his divine rights. Sakharam calls the husbands who take out their frustration on their wives as "impotent", "swine" and "gutless breed". Yet he is a victim of the same fate because that is ultimately what the system does to the human spirit. Sakharam was an antidote to the image of romantic hero. Yet he also laid bare the politics of ownership, property and right of possession. His ideological perception of his relation with the women he keeps in his house is not at all different from that of a regular husband. He insists that in his house he is the king, his wish is and should be the command for the women, his physical and sexual needs must be satisfied as a duty in exchange for the protection he provides (Otherwise who would have kept you in the house) along with food, shelter, clothing (two saris a year) and expects total compliance in return.

"Once a woman is thrown out nobody calls her respectable. Remember that I at least took you in" he tells Laxmi.

But the contractual arrangement between him and the woman he keeps represents a replica of the arrangements in marriage. Here all the romance and glamour of marriage evaporates under the terrible scrutiny of Tendulkar's critical eye. Laxmi's calling him her husband and her subsequent elevation of him into a "God" demonstrates the patterns of thinking instilled in women by the patriarchal tradition. In a sense, this makes the murder of Champa at his hands inevitable. Nothing human can survive the murderous tentacles of these institutions. What shocks the audience is not the fate of Laxmi, Champa and Sakharam but the ugly reality of moral deprivation and corruption that seeps within the soul in the institution of marriage as it exists in the society today. It is an institution in which sexual relationship for a woman is possible only if the self is forgotten in the stupor of alchohol, pleasure is possible only through inflicting pain on the other and "self awareness" is nothing but the mute and moron like acceptance of inhuman subordination or supremacy. Sakharam, Laxmi, Champa are all victims of this familial ideology........."

Tendulkar imagined such a possibility of living together without marriage way back in 1972, which right now has become the latest trend in India, especially flourished in metropolitan cities, which is known as Live-In- Relationship. Even recently inspired by such trend of younger generation, the renowned director Yash Chopra produced a film "**Salam Namste**". In such a relation man and woman live together for certain years and when fed up with each other, they can separate without any claim on the other. In metropolitan cities many young people have accepted "Live-inrelationship" and try to escape from the bondages of marriage. When Tendulkar wrote this play he never imagined that it would become a new culture in 21st century. When this drama was performed, it created uproar in the society because people could not imagine such a relationship between man and woman without marriage. They found such a relation as a danger for the society but now-a-days it becomes the new culture of the so called sophisticated, educated society in big cities.

Tendulkar imagined such a new concept as he felt disillusioned about the institution of marriage in which a wife can be deserted by a husband for trivial reasons. If the marriage is the main pillar of the society, the husband should never desert the wife. But the society is male-dominated and the woman is thrown out from the house for various reasons. Still the deserted woman regards her husband as her god till she dies and a man like Sakharam who becomes her saviour remains a "man" for her as long as they live together.

But the new concept of Sakharam is also not the ideal one. It also does not offer any security or safety to woman. Sakharam does not want to get united to any woman by observing the social ritual of marriage. The role which he expects form Laxmi and Champa is that of an ideal, submissive and faithful wife.

For the smooth running of life compromise, adjustment, adaptability, pulling on, trust, understanding and the quality of forgive and forget are required. Only then the life becomes happy for any couple living together through the institution of marriage or the Live-In-Relationship.

7. DRAMATIC TECHNIQUES IN
SAKHARAM BINDER

For Sakharam Binder, Tendulkar was accused of deliberately choosing sensational themes to get cheap publicity, of writing a crude, non-artistic play that had destroyed the sanctity of the Marathi stage. Tendulkar was shocked by the viciousness of the attacks against him. He admits in an interview that he had expected the play to be ignored by the mainstream, cast aside by critics as yet another failed attempt of his, and rejected by the audience. "Every play is not for everybody". he says, "Those who like what a play has to say, like the play ; those who don't like it's content, don't like it." As for artistry, he says, "A play is a work of art when it reveals its theme and essence exclusively through its mode and attendant detailing rather than through statement and speech." Sakharam Binder fulfills these criteria, and therefore is an artistic play.

Tendulkar has employed certain devices in the writing of this play to make it artistic. Those devices are in the form of an object, character and talking to insects. It seems that Tendulkar felt the need of such devices either to reflect the mental landscape of his characters or to juxtapose the opposite situation. The first device is in form of an object – **A Mridanga** which Sakharam has been shown playing frequently in the play. Not that he is a great lover of music or man given to the field of fine arts so he beats that Mridanga. In fact it is a dramatic technique to display before the spectators the subconscious and unconscious mind of Sakharam. His suppressed desires, dissatisfaction and anguish are given an outlet in the form of that act of beating the Mridanga. It reflects either his extreme unhappiness or dissatisfaction with the situation in which he finds himself. It is shown that Sakharam loves his mridanga and chillum and plays on his mridanga after having his heart's fill of ganja, and then he falls into a trance. It's ironical that this man who has the aesthete in him, is still capable of shocking cruelty towards his women. It is here that Tendulkar lets us have a peep into the inherent lust in men, which brooks no resistance, the insatiable "appetite" in Sakharam's words. The function which cannot be performed with the help of so many words has been performed with a single object with this Mridanga. Mridanga expresses his happiness when he beats it for the first time after Laxmi's arrival. The same Mridanga expresses his mental crisis when he beats it for the second time in course of the play, finding himself torn between two women Champa and Laxmi. It is an additional achievement of Tendulkar that with the same device, two opposite moods of the protagonist are reflected. Mridanga also conveys the idea of Sakharam's timidity because what he can not do in reality, is done by him with that Mridanga. When he fails to control Champa, he conceals his failure by beating that Mridanga.

The scene of Ganpati Puja is one more device employed by Tendulkar in order to make the play effective. The scene of Ganpati Puja is introduced in the play to juxtapose world outside Sakharam's house and inside his house. Of course the presence of the scene gives the glimpse of Marathi culture because Ganpati Puja is an inevitable part of that culture. In fact, Ganpati Puja outside his house and the culture which prevails inside his house are reflecting ,his interior and exterior. Outwardly he participates in the Puja but inwardly he remains the same – lustful fellow, changing his partners frequently.

Laxmi's conversation with ant is the most striking device used by Tendulkar in this play. One comes across such a scene rarely in which a human being is making an attempt to talk to a creature. It happens only in case of extreme happiness or extreme sorrow. Laxmi's case is of an extreme sad condition. She can talk to insects but she fails to have a live relationship with Sakharam with whom she lives. It can also be viewed as an insect can understand a human being. This tragic state of human relationship in the modern times has been brought to the surface through the device of Laxmi's talking to ant. Of course, at the level of reality it remains unresponded by an ant. But the meaning which it conveys, reaches successfully to the spectators.

The frequent appearance of Dawood in the play is also a dramatic device of Tendulkar to indicate the frequent changes of moods in Sakharam. Dawood appears on both the types of occasions in Sakharam's life – when Sakharam is happy after the arrival of Laxmi, Dawood comes and congratulates him and when Sakharam is in the state of crisis because of Champa and Laxmi there is an appearance of Dawood. In fact, within those several appearances which he has in this play. It is the role of a commentator on Sakharam's personal life. He is a friend, a traitor and also a commentator.

Sometimes he is playing the role of an advisor to Sakharam. The presence of Dawood shows the purpose of curiosity, suspense and thrill in the play. His character has in it several shades of human personality at a time. Dawood's character makes "Sakharam Binder" more interesting and relevant to the culture today. His character indicates that one who is a friend and an adviser can also be a traitor because human mind is unpredictable. Such devices of Tendulkar in the play make it more enjoyable and relevant.

8. CONCLUSION

None can deny the fact that literature of every time and space springs from the cultural ethos of that time and space. The natural accordance is always to be found between the literature of a particular time, space and society of that time and space. Literature springs from culture and hence with all its aesthetics it proves to be a social and cultural document of that particular time and space. The bond between literature and culture is an everlasting phenomenon. The basic reason why this tuning is to be found between literature and the cultural ethos is the commitment of the writer. Writer experiences a greater commitment to his time and space and writes with a vision of reality as well as responsibility. His aim is to see and sees the prevailing norms of his culture in a real sense of the term and so he becomes a committed person, a committed writer. His status as a writer would be futile if there is no sense of responsibility or tone of commitment in his works. The first thing that can be concluded on the basis of the present research work on Vijay Tendulkar's plays is that he is a playwright with a conscious sense of commitment. A writer who desires to be aesthetic in his approach of writing, should in no way give himself a consent to connive at the prevailing realities of his time, culture and society. Tendulkar remains faithful not only in observing those realities but also in displaying them through his plays. He is a dramatist with commitment to his time and country. His plays are adorned with aesthetic value but he does not try to escape from his commitment. It can be justified more elaborately on the basis of his plays.

As a playwright he holds a mirror through his works before the society which is very much Indian and the society finds its own reflection in that mirror. Nothing of Society – good and evil, high and low, black and white – remains, unseen or unnoticed to him. His plays present before the spectators both the sides of life of an average Indian.

Tendulkar as a playwright reflects both the sides of Indian life – the bright side as well as the dark one. As Gouri Ramanarayan aptly observes "with his exposure to Marathi theatre form childhood and journalistic background Vijay Tendulkar turned contemporary socio-political situation into explosive drama". He has dwelt on the alienation of the modern individual, satirized contemporary politics, forcefully depicted social and individual tensions, portrayed with finesse the complexities of human character and vigorously exploited man-woman relationship in several of his works. Significantly the themes which have engaged his most frequent attention, have been the plight of woman in a maledominated urban middle class society, and the husband-wife relationship as obtained in metropolitan centers like Bombay and Delhi. Vijay Tendulkar portrays the contemporary society and the predicament of man in it with a special focus on the morbidity in his plays. His plays touch almost every aspect of human life in the modern world and share the disillusionment of the post- modern intellectuals. However, he seems to highlight three major issues: gender, power and violence.

A close study of Vijay Tendulkar's plays reveals that Tendulkar is not a teacher or preacher. He is not one of those dramatists who use their medium in the service of their favourite socio-political ideology. He is not out to propagate any particular philosophy of life. Some critics have pointed out leftist interpretation to the plays like Ghashiram Kotwal, Kamala and Sakharam Binder. It shows that his plays are open to diverse interpretations and cannot be tied down to a single line of thinking. So the question whether Tendulkar writes for life's sake or art's sake is pointless. All that we can say is that he seems to favour socialist humanism but it should also be remembered that his plays do not revolve in the orbit of that ideology either.

It is significant to note most of Tendulkar's plays are gyno-centric. He was essentially dealing with a world, which in the guise of the modern ideal of nuclear family rejected woman's independence as a citizen, enforced traditional Hindu-Brahmin norms of behavior, crushed her attempts of gaining freedom and exercised a rigid control on her sexuality and productivity.

Sakharam Binder centers round the issue of gender, latent violence and sex in human mind and acceptance of woman merely as body by man. It is probably Tendulkar's most naturalistic play. Sociologists may claim that marriage is an institution and religion may claim that marriage is a holy knot but by and large it has declined to the level of a contract and compromise in which man finds himself free to change the partner as and when he desires. This bitter truth of recent times demands courage for its manifestation which has been done by Vijay Tendulkar. The play grew around the central character Sakharam, a binder, who became the antithesis of the ideal view of his caste that is Brahmin. Sakharam lives with a woman who either left or was left by her man on contractual cohabitation. Though he proclaims that his house represents an alternative to marriage, actually the system is just like marriage shorn of all the romantic trapping. His ideological perception of his relation with the women he keeps in his house is not at all different from that of a regular husband. His physical and sexual needs must be satisfied as a duty in exchange for the protection he provides. Sakharam is to be seen as the product of patriarchal tyranny at home. He is a victim of the bad script written on his tender mind in his early childhood by his psychopathic parents. He wants to rebel against the inhuman traditions but paradoxically enough, he proves worse than a traditional husband.

In Silence! Sakharam Binder and the Vultures, Tendulkar deals with the unconventional theme of sex and violence, but a shift in his concerns is evident when he professes emphatically that man is constantly and violently seeking after positions of power and he would work on this "basic theme" hereafter. In fact, he became aware of moral values in the modern political system. His dramatic creation reflects his concern for common man who, caught in the matrix of opportunistic ethics of modern world, feels alienated. **Ghashiram Kotwal** shows how a common man hero, seeking, power, confronts the people who are already in power and undergoes an organic change. Though, it is based on historical legend, is not actually a historical play. Unlike other dramatists Tendulkar finds a parallel running between antiquity and modernity.

The analysis of Vijay Tendulkar's plays show that his commitment remains the same in each of his plays. His plays put forth burning issues of the contemporary society and times without allowing himself to interfere. He presents on the stage characters as free individuals who live according to their inner will and inner landscape that gives the touch of reality to his plays. Nowhere his characters sound as puppets in his hands. They live, love and suffer because of their own way of life. They are round and dynamic in nature, whether they remain for short or long span of time before the audience. Tendulkar believed that the playwright needs to be an actor-writer who plays 'roles' as he writes, and it helped Tendulkar in depicting the characters as he was associated with the theatre. According to him characterization in a play is to a large extent revealed through the dialogue. Therefore the playwright must have a mouldable and not a rigid style of writing. He must change his style with every character and Tendulkar as a playwright followed this.

Each of his characters reveals a new pattern of characterization. Sakharam represents the impotent fury of male masochism. Ramakant and Umakant present vulturine instinct of human beings'avarice, cunningness, lust, ruthlessness. Ghashiram represents lust for Power. Jaisingh Jadav's character is study of success-oriented modern man. Mr. Nath of "Kanyadaan" represents Ganadhian ideology. His women characters truly exemplify Santa Gokhale's remark that they are romanticized, idealized or forced to live by their creator's symbolic purposes. They are first and foremost human beings of flesh and blood who drew their features from the widest range of observed examples. They are allowed to inhabit the entire spectrum for the unbelievably gullible to the clever, from the malleable to the stubborn, from the conservative to the rebellious, from the self-sacrificing to the grasping. Leela Benare, Manik, Champa, Seva, are unconventional heroines, whereas Laxmi, Rama, Kamala, Sarita, Lalita Gauri, Jyoti, Mrs. Kashikar appear as victims in the patriarchal world.

"Theatre is a visual medium as much as it is a medium of words. This visual aspect needs to be used properly not only to create a relief in the barrage of continuously emoted words but also to provide powerful visual insights into the complex content of the play. A play staged in a theater is not a radio play to be heard with closed eyes and enjoyed. The visual element in a stage play, if not used properly can work against the magic of words and harm the play."

A play has a structure. Structure does not mean the plot or the story of the play. It is a framework. It is not visible but is felt." These views of Tendulkar enabled him to remain "experimental" in his plays. Even in commercial drama he made room for himself and had maintained his uniqueness. His plays reveal his art in maintaining economy of words, the ability to express maximum meaning in minimum words. His use of language is marked by an intelligent use of the punctuation marks, blank spaces, full stops and exclamation marks are effectively used by him. The play within the play technique in "Silence! The Court is in session" for the first time in Marathi drama opened up a new height of Drama. In "Kamala" the motif of the hectic phone calls, the device of the fading of lights, suggesting, in an oblique fashion are worth noting.

The success or failure of any work of art depends upon its appeal – whether that appeal proves to be transitory or everlasting. A work of art with an everlasting appeal always remains eternal. It will not be out of the way or excessive exaggeration if the same thing is said about Tendulkar's plays. We do notice even today victims like Kamala, Benare, Sarita, Rama, Lalita Guari in Society. At the same time we notice even today males likes Arun, Sakharam, Ramakant and Umakant, Jaisingh Jadav, Ghashiram etc. as long as such characters are there in our society, the appeal of his plays would remain intact. His plays will never lose the quality of relevance with which they have been written.

BIBLIOGRAPHY

PRIMARY SOURCES

- **Tendulkar, Vijay** – *Collected Plays in Translation,* (Oxford University Press, 2003.)

- **Tendulkar, Vijay** – *Ghashiram Kotwal,* Seagull Books, Calcutta, 2002

SECONDARY SOURCES

- **Abrams M.H.** *"A Glossary of Literary Terms"* Macmillian. 1996

- **Abrams Teera**, *"Folk Theatre in Maharashtrian Social Development programme,"* Educational Theatre Journal 1975

- **Babu M.R.** *Political Deformity, In Indian drama Today,* Prestige - Books – 1990

- **Babu M.S.** *"Spiritual Deformity,"* In Indian Drama Today, Prestige Books – 1990.

- **Babu, Sarat M.** *"Indian Drama Today",* New Delhi, Prestige Books, 1997

- **Banerjee Arundhati**, *Introduction Five plays by Vijay Tendulkar ,* Oxford up, Bombay

- **Bhalla M. M,** *"Folk Theatre and operas",* A Handful of Dreams Kantas Book Depot, 1977, Delhi.

- **Bhasin Kamala & Khan Nighat** Said *"Some questions on Feminism and its relevance in South Asia,"* ISBN New Delhi - 1993.

- **Bhatnagar M.K.** *"Indian writings in English"* Atlantic publishers, New Delhi.

- **Bhatnagar M.K.,** *Feminist English Literature,* Atlantic Publishers New Delhi

- **Bhave Pushpa** *"Vijay Tendulkar : A Study in Contemporary Indian Theatre",* Sangit Natak Akademi, New Delhi – 1989.

- **Bhayani Utpal** – *સામાજિક નાટક, એક નૂતન ઉન્મેષ: વિજય તેંડુલકર,* NavBharat Sahitya Mandir 1993.

- **Das Bijay Kumar** – *Critical Essay on post-colonial literature,* Atlantic Publishers.- 2001

- **Das Bijay kumar.** *"Comparative Literature,"* Atlantic Publishers, New Delhi.

- **Deshpande G.P** *"Modern Indian Drama,"* An Anthology, Sahitya Akademi, New Delhi 2002

- **Dharan N.S.** *"The plays of Vijay Tendulkar"* Creative Books – New Delhi – 1999

- **Dharan N.S.** *"The Plays of Vijay Tendulkar",* Creative Books, 1999

- **Dhawan R.K.** *"20 years of Indian writing",* IAES, New Delhi 1999.

- **Dodiya J.K. & Surendran K.V.** *"Indian English Drama, Critical Perspectives,"* Sarup & Sons – 2002

- **Gargi, Balwant.** *Theatre in India,* New York: Theatre Arts, 1962.

- **Gayle Greene and Coppelia Kahn,** *"Feminist scholarship and the Social construction of woman,"* Making a Difference : Feminist Literary criticism, London, Methuen – 1985.

- **George, K.M., ed.** *Comparative Indian Literature,* Madras: Macmillan, 1984.

- **Gowda, Anniah.** *Indian Drama,* Mysore: Univ. of Mysore, 1974.

- *વષ્ણકર ભી. ન – અનુસંધાન, ગુર્જર એજન્સી, ગાંધીમાર્ગ, અમદાવાદ.*

- *વષ્ણકર ભી.ન. – નવોન્મેષ, ભગવતી ઓફસેટ , અમદાવાદ*

- *વષ્ણકર ભી. ન. – દલિત સાહિત્ય, પૂનમ ઓફસેટ, ગાંધીનગર*

- **Jyenger, K.R.S.,** *Indian writing in English,* Sterling publishers – 1985. New Delhi

- **Karnad Girish** *"Author's Introduction,"* Three Plays, Oxford University press, Delhi, 1994.

- **Karnad Girish** *"Nag Mandal"* & *"Hayavadana,"* Oup – 1993.

- **Kumar, Geeta** *"Portrayal of Women in Tendulkar's Shintata Court Chalu Ahe,"* New Directions in Indian Drama. New Delhi, Prestige – 1994.

- **M. Sarat Babu** *"Vijay Tendulkar's Ghashiram Kotwal,"* A Reader's Companion, Asia book Club – New Delhi – 2003.

- **Madge V.M.-** *Vijay Tendulkar's Plays: An Anthology of Recent Criticism,* Pencraft International, 2007

- **Mehta Jay** – *Zankhi: Glimpse of Marathi Drama and Literature,* Unique offset

- **Naik M.K.** *"A History of Indian English Literature,"* Sahitya Akademi, New Delhi – 1982

- **Naik M.K. and Mokashi S. Punekar**, *Perspectives on Indian Drama in English,* Oxford UP – 1977, Madras

- **Pandey S. and Freya Barwa** – *New Directions in Indian Drama* Prestige Books.

- **Reddy, Bayapa P.** *Studies in Indian writing English with a Focus on Indian English Drama,* New Delhi: Prestige, 1990.

- **Reddy, Venkata K.** *Critical Studies in Commonwealth Literature,* New Delhi: Prestige, 1994.

- **Sarat Babu M.** – *Vijay Tendulkar's Ghashiram Kotwal,* Asia Book Club, 2003

- **Sharma Vinod Bala** *"Critical Perspectives Ghashiram Kotwal"* Asia book club- 2001.

- **Sharma Vinod Bala** *"Critical Perspectives Ghasiram Kotwal",* Asia Book Club, 2001

- **Shiply Joseph J.** *Dictionary of World Literary Terms,* New Delhi: Doaba House, 1993.

- **Srinivas M.N. ,** *Social change in Modern India,* Orient Longman – 1972

- **Surendran K.V.** *"Indian Writing : Critical perspectives Sarup & Sons."* New Delhi

- **Taraporewala Freya and Pandey Sudhakar** *"Contemparary Indian Drama,"* New Delhi, Prestige Book - 1990

- **Tendulkar Vijay** *Katha* – 2001

- **Vatsyaya, Kapila.** *Traditional Indian Theatre:* Multiple Streams, New Delhi: National Book trust, 1980.

- **Veena Noble Dass** – *"Studies in Contemporary Indian Drama,"* Prestige – 1990.

ARTICLES FROM NEWSPAPERS

- **Rajadhyaksha Mukta**, Times of India – Monday, January 29, 2007., "Times review / Book Mark., "Vijay Tendulkar answers Some questions."

- **Times News Network** "Times of India" Tuesday, May 20, 2008.

- **The Hindu** 3/10/04., The Hindu - Sunday, September 16, 2001.

WEB SOURCES

http://www.rediff.com/news/2008/may/19vijay.htm (died article)

http://www.imdb.com/name/nm0854919/ (biography)

http://en.wikipedia.org/wiki/Vijay_Tendulkar (biography)

http://www.littleindia.com/news/123/ARTICLE/3138/2008-07-15.html (By:

Shekhar Hattangadi)

http://www.hinduonnet.com/thehindu/mag/2005/11/06/stories/2005110600310500.htm (**A rich tapestry of women's stories**) Sunday, Nov 06, 2005 on kamala

http://salaamtheatre.org/kamala2004.html

www.urdutech.net/.../2008/05/vijaytendulkar.jpg

chat.indiatimes.com/articleshow/753698.cms

www.sajaforum.org/2008/05/obit-vijay-tend.html

http://news.bbc.co.uk/2/hi/south_asia/7407808.stm (death article)

www.hindu.com/.../stories/2007012002590800.htm (ghasiram) (Saturday, Jan 20, 2007)

http://www.hindu.com/mp/2007/01/20/images/2007012002590801.jpg

http://kpowerinfinity.spaces.live.com/Blog/cns!EEA9A8ECBFC1B50B!309.entry (((kanyadaan performance article) (August 11

Vijay Tendulkar's 'Kanyadaan' - An Unparalleled Performance)

www.indiaclub.com/shop/AuthorSelect.asp?Autho... (kanyadaan poster)

http://geekydood.wordpress.com/2008/04/30/silence-the-court-is-in-session/

http://www.quillandink.netfirms.com/Theatrecian/tcreview060506.htm (silence)

www.alibris.com/.../author/Tendulkar,%20Vijay (image)

http://timesofindia.indiatimes.com/articleshow/23796750.cms (article on ghasiram kotwal's performance) (30 Sep 2002, 2309)

http://picasaweb.google.com/suman.nsd/100MEDIA#5196466031138807074 (ghasiram kotwal)

http://www.mumbaitheatreguide.com/dramas/hindi/sakharam_binder_retold.asp (sakharam binder , performance article and photo)

http://www.sepiamutiny.com/sepia/archives/000636.html (photo sakharam binder)

http://www.iaac.us/Tendulkarfestival/VijayTendulkar.htm (photo with cast of sakharam binder)

http://www.bookrags.com/wiki/Shantata%21_Court_Chalu_Aahe (silence)

http://www.bookrags.com/wiki/Ghashiram_Kotwal

http://www.bookrags.com/wiki/Sakharam_Binder

http://www.bookrags.com/wiki/Vijay_Tendulkar

http://www.indianexpress.com/res/web/pIe/ie/daily/19991020/ile20071.html (article, Wednesday, October 20, 1999)

http://passionforcinema.com/a-conversation-with-sir-vijay-tendulkar/ (conversation with tendulkar)

http://shreevarma.homestead.com/bookreviews1.html

www.ingramcontent.com/pod-product-compliance
Lightning Source LLC
Chambersburg PA
CBHW071058280326
41928CB00050B/2552